D1388393

Wet Playtimes

Activities that are easy to prepare and
that children will love

Brilliant
PUBLICATIONS

Christine Green

Other Titles in the 100+ Fun Ideas Series:

For further information on all of the above books, please see pages 100–102.

Published by Brilliant Publications
Unit 10, Sparrow Hall Farm
Edlesborough, Dunstable
Bedfordshire, LU6 2ES, UK
www.brilliantpublications.co.uk

Sales and stock enquiries:
Tel: 01202 712910
Fax: 0845 1309300
E-mail: brilliant@bebc.co.uk
General information enquiries:
Tel: 01525 222292

The name Brilliant Publications and the
logo are registered trademarks.

Written by Christine Green
Illustrated by Catherine Ward

© Text Christine Green 2009
© Design Brilliant Publications 2009

ISBN 978-1-905780-32-7
First printed and published in the UK in
2009

The right of Christine Green to be
identified as the author of this work has
been asserted by herself in accordance
with the Copyright, Designs and Patents
Act 1988.

Contents

Wet Playtimes

Introduction

This book was written with both teacher (or lunchtime supervisor) and pupil in mind; to educate, entertain and also provide useful ways to keep pupils amused when those inevitable wet playtime breaks occur – when everyone has to remain indoors and fifteen minutes can seem like a lifetime to children, and an eternity to the teacher.

Undoubtedly, play is central to a growing child's development and has a fundamental role in their lives. It teaches them:

✦   About their world and the things in it
✦   To integrate with their peers
✦   To accept failure as well as success
✦   Other ways of expressing their feelings and emotions
✦   Through play, children learn that they can be whatever they want to be.

This book will demonstrate to teachers, and those involved in educating young children, that education can, and should, have an element of fun integrated into it, even during those wet break times.

Most of the following games can easily be adapted to suit the age of the children in question. The main thing to remember while doing these activities is that the object is to have fun!

We have used the word 'teacher' to refer to the adult organizing the activity. They could be done by teaching assistants, lunchtime supervisors, after-school leaders, scout leaders or anyone else working with groups of children.

Most of the games can easily be adapted for use throughout the day. You don't need to wait for a rainy day to use them!

Pen and paper games

Word games create a host of opportunities for considered thinking and enhancing a child's oral communication. They can encourage a child's interest in both the spoken and written word, which in turn will help develop their ability to use words more confidently in their everyday life. There are clear links to literacy work. For example, *Dictionary race* (Activity 8), will help to develop dictionary skills and *Take a letter* (Activity 25) will help to develop listening and writing skills.

Drawing can also develop descriptive and communicative skills. In *Ruler of the country* (Activity 15), the children have to design a flag and *Blindfold drawing* (Activity 16) will help to develop spacial skills.

Wet Playtimes

1. Name game

✦ The teacher thinks of a word (eg, gate) which each child writes across the top of their paper in large well-spaced letters. Down the side of the paper they write four or five categories, eg countries, girls' names, boys' names and a fruit.

✦ Each child must then write down as many words relating to those categories beginning with the different letters within a time of three minutes.

✦ One point is awarded for every word and two points if no-one else has thought of it. An example:

	G	A	T	E
Countries	Greece	Austria	Thailand	Egypt
Girls' names	Grace	Alice	Toni	Elizabeth
Boys' names	Graham	Alan	Thomas	Edward
Fruit	Grape	Apple	Tomato	Eggfruit

girl's name

country

fruit

boy's name

2. **Hangman**

✦   A game played between two children or as a class to help improve their spelling.

✦   Player one chooses a familiar word/phrase and each letter of the word/phrase is represented by a dash, and written down on the paper. If there are several words (ie, television set) then a forward slash(/) should be inserted in between the words.

✦   Underneath the 'mystery word' player one draws a gallows (see the diagram) but the body (hangman) is only drawn when the game begins.

✦   There are several ways to play Hangman but this is the most traditional and easiest method for young children to follow.

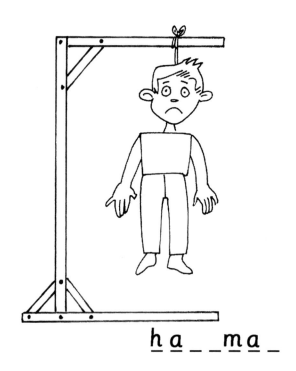

h a _ _ m a _

- Player two must try to guess the identity of the word/phrases and in order to do this can say one letter at a time. If that letter has been used in any word then, wherever it appears, player one must write the letter on top of the dash.

- However, if the letter does not appear in any of the word(s) one body part can be added to the gallows. To begin with 1) head attached to the short downward line then 2) eyes 3) ears 4) nose 5) mouth 6) hair 7) body 8) legs and9) arms.

- If at any time player two thinks they can identify the word(s) they can take a guess. If the drawing is completed before the word(s) are guessed then player one wins the game.

- Tip – when younger children are playing it is often a good idea to write the alphabet across the top of the page and cross out each letter as it is called.

3. Mixed-up stories

- Give each pupil a piece of paper. Ask pupils to write the first few lines of a story. They then should fold the paper over, so that only the last line of their writing is showing.

- Each pupil then hands the paper to another child, who then has to write the next bit of the story. When they have finished, they fold up the paper so that only their last line is showing, and the paper passes on to yet another child.

- Pass each paper to four or five children. The last pupil should try to write the ending to the story.

- Then open the stories up and have fun reading them!

4. **Mystery person**

✦ One child is chosen to come to the front of the classroom.

✦ That person must then secretly choose another class member but only whisper the identity to the teacher.

✦ They then have three minutes in which to relate as much physical information as they can about their mystery person to the rest of the class – are they tall or short, hair colour, type of shoes they wear; in fact anything except revealing their name.

✦ Using the description given the children have five minutes to draw a picture of the person that has been described on their paper.

✦ The fun begins when each pupil has to stand up and show the class their own picture of how they perceive the mystery person to look. At this point the player can reveal the true identity and the winner is decided by the teacher (the closest likeness).

✦ Tips – to make it more fun, the chosen mystery person could be someone else in the school who the children know such as the headteacher, a teaching assistant or a school secretary.

5. Anagram fun

✦ Decide on a topic, some ideas are: toys, drinks, food, animals. Write it down on the whiteboard. Underneath note down ten anagrams of certain objects found within that category.

✦ For example, the chosen topic may be fruit. Write down ten different fruits in anagram form on the whiteboard. For instance, reap (pear), cheap (peach), no gear (orange), peal P (apple).

✦ The children are then given five minutes to unscramble as many words as they can and write them down on their paper.

✦ One point is awarded for every correct word and the winner(s) are those who have successfully unscrambled the most.

✦ Tip – for older children make up anagrammed sentences whereby the sets of words are given on a piece of paper and the students then have to build them into a significant sentence within a space of time.

6. Ready steady go

✦ The children have to write down as much information as they can about themselves, including the colour of hair/eyes, any brothers/sister/pets.

✦ After five minutes the children exchange their paper with a classmate who then has to read out whatever information is written down to the rest of the class and then count up the number of words used.

✦ The winner is the person who has written the most words.

7. **Word hunt**

✦ The teacher writes a word containing at least ten letters on the whiteboard.

✦ Each child has five minutes to write down as many different words as they can only using the letters in the word once.

✦ For example, the chosen word may be 'celebration'. The children then have to think up as many words as they can out of the letters within that word, such as tin, rate, tribe.

✦ At the end of the time each child has to read out their list. One point is awarded for every word, two points if no-one else has thought of it.

✦ Rules – all words must contain three or more letters and be found in the dictionary; spelling should be correct and no abbreviations or names can be used.

8. **Dictionary race**

✦ Encouraging children to use a dictionary can seem an almost impossible task, but not if it is integrated into a game.

✦ The teacher writes a list of twelve unfamiliar words on the whiteboard and the children are given five minutes to find the definitions in the dictionary and write them down on a piece of paper.

✦ When the time is up the person who finds the most correct definitions is the winner.

9. **Obscure words**

✦ The teacher writes down ten occupations the children may not have heard of (ie, geologist, pharmacist, and dietician).

✦ Working in pairs or groups the children have ten minutes, using whatever resources available (dictionaries, encyclopaedias, magazines, newspapers, the Internet), to find out a brief description of each job and write their answers down on the paper.

✦ Two points are awarded for each correct answer.

✦ Tip – it does not have to be limited to jobs.

10. Parts of speech

✦ This is a great game for teaching the parts of speech, but it will need some preparation.

✦ First of all write a paragraph or two about an interesting topic (or copy one from a book). Blank out some of the words, to form a 'close test', but write underneath the part of speech needed (eg noun, verb, adverb, adjective, etc).

✦ Without reading the story, tell the children the part of speech needed and ask the children to supply a word. Write their suggestion in the blank. Go through the whole passage in this way.

✦ When you have finished, read what is sure to be a hilarious story to the class.

✦ This game can also be played in pairs or small groups, with one child taking the role of the teacher. If you prepare several passages, they can all take a turn.

11. **Steeple climb**

✦ This is a fun game that can be played independently, or in groups.

✦ The idea is that all players begin with one letter, ie E, and from that letter they have to build a steeple adding a new letter each time.

✦ Whoever builds the highest steeple in three minutes with legitimate words, is the winner.

12. **Study that picture!**

✦ Attach a large picture to the whiteboard, or display one on an interactive whiteboard, and give the children three minutes to study it.

✦ The fun begins when you remove the picture and in one minute they have to write down as much information as they can remember about the picture and report it to the rest of the class.

✦ One point is awarded for each thing they remember and the winner is whoever has the most points at the end with no repetitions.

13. **Jigsaw words**

✦ Write down 20 words which the children would recognize on pieces of card. Photocopy, laminate and cut them out.

✦ Cut each of the cards in half again so you end up with half the letters on each piece, eg if the word were 'parent' then 'par' would be on one card and 'ent' on the other.

✦ Split the class into teams, give them each a pack of cards. They have five minutes in which to match up as many words as they can.

✦ The team that has matched up the most words correctly at the end of the game is the winner.

14. First finished

✦ Write the alphabet on the whiteboard and highlight only one letter.

✦ On a piece of paper each child draws out three columns titled with the name of a country, a girl/boy's first name and a wild animal. Then underneath they have two minutes in which to write down as many countries, girl's names and wild animals they can think of beginning with whichever letter has been highlighted.

✦ At the end of that round each child must stand up and read out their list, two points are awarded for words that no-one else has got and one extra point if it has been spelt correctly.

✦ Example: AB C DEFGHIJKLMNOPQRSTUVWXYZ

Write down three categories on the top of the paper:

Name of a country:	Girl's first name:	Animal
Canada	Catherine	Cheetah
Croatia	Chelsea	Cat

✦ Round two begins when the teacher highlights another letter.

15. **Ruler of the country**

✦ This game can be adapted to suit all ages, there are no winners or losers – just a lot of fun guaranteed!

✦ Provide each child with a sheet of paper and some crayons, tell them to imagine that they are King or Queen of their very own country and so have to design a flag.

✦ Leave them for ten minutes after which time each child comes to the front of the classroom to talk about their country flag, why they chose those colours, the name of the country, any laws they have prepared.

✦ The class teacher could display the most interesting and well thought out design on the classroom wall and perhaps incorporate it into a future geography lesson.

16. Blindfold drawing

✦ Ask the children to write down the name of an object for drawing. Encourage them to choose something quite simple such as an apple, a flower or a house. Put the slips of paper into a bag for selection later.

✦ Divide the class into two teams and choose two pupils, one from each team, to come to the whiteboard where they will select a slip of paper from the bag, be blindfolded and then given a marker to draw their object.

✦ Both children have three minutes in which to draw the object that they selected.

✦ At the end of the time they may remove their blindfold and whoever has got the closest image is awarded two points for their team.

✦ Keep a tally of points scored as each child takes their turn.

17. **Who is it?**

✦ Each child is given two minutes to write down on piece of paper three bits of information about themselves such as I have black hair, I have a pet mouse, I wear brown shoes. They can write anything except their name.

✦ The paper is folded and collected by the teacher who then slips them into a cardboard box. One by one the children go to the front of the classroom, pick out a piece of paper and read whatever details are written down before trying to guess the identity of the person.

✦ If they are successful in identifying the anonymous person the paper is thrown away, but if they can't guess who it is within 60 seconds the paper has to be replaced into the box and it is the turn of another pupil.

18. **Secret drawing**

✦ Draw ten large squares on a piece of paper and photocopy sufficient sheets, one for each pupil.

✦ The aim of the game is that each child has ten minutes to draw a different picture in each of those squares and identify them. However, all the pictures must somehow be related to one another.

✦ For example, a TV set in one square, a table in another, a chair in another – what do they share in common – all can be found in the living room of a house. Other ideas could be sporting equipment, items of clothing, objects in the park or at the beach.

✦ At the end each child stands up to talk to the rest of the class about their pictures.

✦ Each illustration that is drawn and correctly identified is awarded two points but if there is a picture which has no relation to the others, or for which the child can't give an explanation, it is then eliminated from the game.

✦ The winner – whoever scores the highest number of points.

19. **Decipher the code**

✦ Children love playing detectives and with this game they really can act out the role of secret agent.

✦ Write the alphabet down on a sheet of paper and underneath write it again but backwards. For example:

A	B	C	D	E	F	G	H	I	J
Z	Y	X	W	V	U	T	S	R	Q

K	L	M	N	O	P	Q	R	S	T
P	O	N	M	L	K	J	I	H	G

U	V	W	X	Y	Z
F	E	D	C	B	A

✦ Photocopy enough sheets for each child. On the whiteboard write out a secret message (using the backwards alphabet) and give the class ten minutes to try to decipher it.

✦ Children who have successfully completed the message at the end can read it out to the rest of the class and one point is awarded for each word: two points for those who have the spelling correct and an extra point for those who have remembered to include any punctuation.

20. **Smile**

✦ Cut out lots of round smiley circles from cardboard.

✦ Draw a large happy smiley face on the whiteboard with a slogan: 'Make me smile today'.

✦ Start off a class discussion about what makes people smile, talk about the number of facial muscles used in order to create this action, how smiling and laughter is good for you, talk about the difference between a laugh and a smile.

✦ Give children a smiley circle and ask them to draw in their own happy face and then write underneath what it is that makes them smile. As a happy reminder, pin the smiley faces up around the classroom wall.

21. **Spell as they sound**

✦ Writing down some words according to how they sound can read total nonsense for example: 'ten issues' (but if you read the two words quickly you will find that the words sound like 'tennis shoes').

✦ This is challenging but great fun, and a game children will thoroughly enjoy attempting to pit their wits against, especially if given a clue about the category of the word(s).

✦ Some examples to use:

Words	Clue	Identity
Win Stun Church Hill	Famous historical person	WINSTON CHURCHILL
Tray See Bee Cur	TV programme/book	TRACY BEAKER
Sid Knee	Capital city	SYDNEY
Sand Tackle Laws	Fictional person	SANTA CLAUS
Aisle Oh View	Phrase	I LOVE YOU

✦ See how many new ones the children can come up with; the most original ones win one point.

22. **Getting ahead**

✦ Each pupil is given a piece of paper and told to draw the head of a human being, a bird or an animal. The paper is then folded over to hide the drawing and then passed to the next person who has to draw a body, again it could be the body of an animal, a bird or a person, anything they choose.

✦ The paper is folded over again, thereby concealing both the head and body parts before being passed to the next person who now must draw in the legs or lower part of the body.

✦ Finally the last person on the table opens the picture to reveal what monster has been created. The winning table is the one to have created the most ghoulish drawing of all.

23. **Think words**

✦ Played individually or with fellow pupils this game encourages children to think about words and gives them confidence to use a dictionary more proficiently.

✦ Write a word vertically down on the whiteboard, preferably one containing seven letters.

✦ Leave a space and directly parallel begin to write that same word again but this time back to front.

✦ For example, if the chosen word is ENGLAND

E	D
N	N
G	A
L	L
A	G
N	N
D	E

✦ The object is for the pupil to think up words, (or look in the dictionary) and find a word that begins, in this case with the letter E and end with the letter D and write it across in the appropriate space. The same format is followed for the remainder of the letters.

✦ One point is awarded for each letter in the words written (and spelled) correctly. Whoever has the most points at the end is the winner. The secret is in trying to think up the longest possible words each time.

◆   The end result might be:

Word	Points awarded
E r r a n D	4
N o u N	2
G a l A	2
L o y a L	3
A g r e e i n G	6
N e o N	2
D a n c E	3

24. Link spelling

✦ The teacher randomly asks a pupil to spell a word. When they have done so the pupil sitting next to them on the table must think of a new word beginning with the last letter of the previous one and spell it out loud.

✦ For example, if the word was 'teacher', the next word will have to begin with the letter 'R'. The game continues around the class from table to table. The only way players are eliminated from the game is if they spell the word incorrectly, repeat a word already been given, or cannot think of a word in ten seconds.

✦ The winner is the last remaining person in the game.

✦ Tip – make it slightly more difficult by keeping the words within a certain category (ie flowers, farm animals, verbs or nouns).

25. Take a letter

✦   Give each child a piece of paper and a pencil. The teacher stands at the front of the class and reads out a simple note. The children have to write down every word spoken.

✦   For example: this is to remind parents that the school will be closed next Tuesday 4th May due to a teacher-training day.

✦   Each child must then stand up and read out the note. It sounds easy but how many actually get it correct?

26. Finding facts

✦   Give each table a famous person from history and in ten minutes they must research by whatever means available as many interesting facts about that person as they can.

✦   The winning table is the one to have found the most facts in that space of time. In the case of a tie, give another two minutes to try to find any others.

27. **Gone shopping**

✦ On the whiteboard write each letter of the alphabet and alongside an amount of money each letter is worth:
A = 1p   B = 2p   C = 3p

✦ Underneath write out a shopping list. The aim is for the children to work out the cost of each item by adding together the values of each letter in that word.

✦ A prime example could be: Apples
A = 1p   P = 16p   P = 16p   L = 12p   E = 5p
S = 19p

✦ The children then write down on their paper the cost of each letter and total them up at the end, ie Apples = 69p.

✦ Using the same principle write down a list of fruit on the whiteboard for the children to copy and then convert letters into numbers and total them up at the end. If it is done correctly there will be several winners at the end of the game with the total amount of their shopping list.

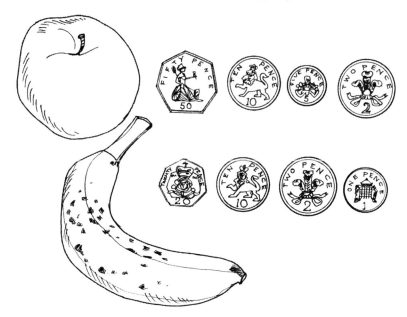

Group Games

Games are a great way of developing interpersonal skills. Through playing games pupils learn to co-operate with each other, take turns and work together as a group.

In this chapter you are sure to find activities to suit every occasion and class.

Most can be done with any age, and for many of the activities, tips are given on how you can adapt the game for different age ranges and abilities.

Some of the games, such as *Wanderers* (Activity 33) and *Teacher portraits* (Activity 48), are just for fun. Others have an element of competition to them.

Sometimes during wet playtimes, what you really need is for the children to be able to use up some pent-up energy. Active games such as *All change* (Activity 31), *Farmer Gill says* (Activity 36) and *Back-to-back* (Activity 35) are ideal for this. At other times you may need a more sedentary activity, to calm pupils down, such as *Box of surprises* (Activity 43) or *Hit* (Activity 39).

27. **Body works**

◆ Draw, laminate and cut out a body shape on to large sheets of card. On separate pieces of smaller card draw, laminate and cut out various parts of the body: two legs, two arms, two feet, two hands, head, eyes, nose, mouth and hair.

◆ Each table is then given a set of the cards and a body outline.

◆ The teacher gives one clue relating to each body part, eg 'you can hop on them' or 'you can use them to throw and catch balls with' (the clues can be made more difficult depending on the age of the children). From this one clue the children have to guess what part of the body it relates to and lay that card alongside.

◆ To make the game more fun give them only 60 seconds in which to find that piece and the first table to have completed their body at the end of the game correctly is the winner.

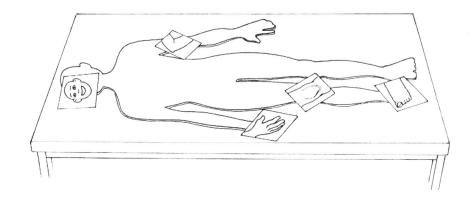

28. **Guess the letter**

✦ This is an easy game to play for young children to help with their alphabet and thinking skills.

✦ The children sit in a circle. The teacher throws a beanbag or a soft ball to one child who must immediately think of a word beginning with the letter 'A', within five seconds, before throwing it to another class member who this time has five seconds to think of a word beginning with the letter 'B'.

✦ The game continues in the same way with the beanbag being passed around the circle, each child thinking of the next letter of the alphabet and a new word.

✦ If anyone cannot think of a word within five seconds or fails to catch the beanbag they must fold their arms. If anyone throws the beanbag to someone who already has had a turn they are out of the game.

✦ Tips – for younger children it is a good idea to write the alphabet on the whiteboard; for older children ask them to spell out the word.

Wet Playtimes

29. **Whispering words**

✦ Divide the class into two teams with each member standing behind their fellow player.

✦ The teacher whispers a word or a phrase to the person at the front of each team who, at the word 'go', must turn around and whisper that word to the person standing behind who in turn must turn around and do the same until the message has travelled down the line. The last person must run up to the teacher and whisper the word or phrase.

✦ Whoever is the quickest team to report back the correct word or phrase is the winner.

✦ Tip – for older children the teacher could whisper a message or a word in a foreign language.

30. Sticking straws

✦ Nerves of steel and a steady hand are the main pieces of equipment needed for this game, which can be played at children's respective tables or in teams, in which case they can sit on the floor.

✦ One person takes a fistful of straws and at the word 'go' must release the straws from a height of about 10cm so they spread out in a pile.

✦ The tricky part comes next when each child has to free one straw without touching or moving any others. If another straw does move, that person misses a turn.

✦ Give the children five minutes to see which team/group has separated the most straws successfully. It might be advisable to have a classroom assistant helping to watch that no cheating goes on!

31. All change

+ Everyone sits in a circle. One child is designated 'Director of Operations' and is given a sheet of paper with a list of different countries. Meanwhile, the rest of the class have a card with the name one of those countries written on it.

+ At any time the 'Director' can call out two countries and whoever is holding those two cards must quickly change seats.

+ As they are doing that the 'Director' must try to intervene and jump into one of the seats before them. If he/she does this then whoever is standing takes on the role of 'Director of Operations'.

+ To make it more fun the 'Director' may call out more than two countries or even 'All change' in which case everyone has to get up and move to another seat. The one attraction about this game is that there is no winner or loser; it's simply good fun.

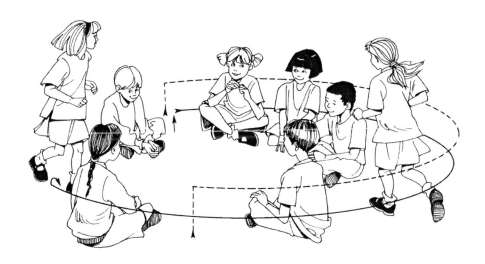

32. **Attention**

✦ This is a superb game for helping young children with their number recognition skills.

✦ A deck of cards is placed facing downwards on the floor. The children sit in a circle and each child is asked a question. It could be on a subject they are studying in class, a spelling or generally based.

✦ If they answer correctly they can turn over two cards and if those two cards match (ie, two 3s) the child keeps them. If they don't match, the cards must be slipped back into the pack again. Should anyone fail to answer the question correctly they simply don't turn over any cards.

✦ The winner is the child to have collected the most cards.

33. Wanderers

◆ Three children are chosen to leave the classroom whilst the rest of the class have to put their heads down on their desks and close their eyes – no peeping!

◆ After a few minutes the three wanderers are allowed back into the classroom where they have to randomly tap the shoulders of three children who in turn must raise a hand in the air.

◆ Once chosen and there are three arms waving in the air the teacher announces game over and those children then have to try to choose which wanderer picked them out.

◆ If they are correct, that person takes over being a wanderer and the game continues.

34. Left, right

◆ This is a simple fun game for children to play in pairs.

◆ Each couple stands three metres apart facing one another. As one player shouts 'Left' the other replies 'Right'.

◆ As they answer one another they place their feet, heel-to-toe and move forwards towards the challenger.

◆ Whoever is the last one to fill the gap with their foot is the winner.

35. **Back-to-back**

✦ This can be a truly challenging game and will delight the children. Divide the class into two teams.

✦ The game begins with two people sat on the floor back to back. The trick is that they have to stand straight up but without using their hands.

✦ Each time they do this successfully another player is added on and by the end of ten minutes the team to have achieved this feat with the most people is the winner.

40

36. **Farmer Gill says**

✦ Loosely based on the game of 'Simon Says' but in this case it is Farmer Gill who gives the instructions, and this time the instructions are related to the noises of farm animals.

✦ The teacher takes on the role of Farmer Gill and the children must obey every instruction he/she gives. For example: Farmer Gill says 'Snort like a pig', Farmer Gill says 'Bleat like a sheep' and so on until all the farm animals you can think of have been done.

✦ If Farmer Gill says 'Roar like a lion', or 'Hiss like a snake', those children who do so are eliminated from the game – because there are no lions or snakes kept on farms!

✦ Tip – older children might like to make 'noises of wild animals', so take them on a safari or 'go on a forest walk' with noises such as an owl hooting, and the sound of twigs crackling.

37. **Action**

✦ The teacher chooses one pupil to whom they whisper an action, which that child has to enact out to their fellow classmates without saying a word.

✦ The first person that recognizes it is the winner but, if after two minutes no one can identify that action, the player continues with another action given by the teacher, until they are eventually caught out.

38. **Listen, listen**

✦ This is a perfect game for demonstrating to children the importance of listening and carrying out instructions.

✦ All the class stand in the middle of the classroom and the teacher reads out the following instructions with which the children have to comply:

If you own a pet at home sit down.
If you have a sister stay standing.
If you have a packed lunch at school stand on one leg.
If you have a brother raise your left hand up.
If you like to eat apples kneel down.
If you like to drink milk sit down.
If you like to read storybooks raise your right hand.
If you like to go for walks stand up.
If you like playing on the computer sit down.
If you like school sit down then stand up.

✦ Lots of different questions can be asked and although there is no outright winner or loser, if someone inadvertently makes a mistake and then realizes it afterwards they are automatically out of the game.

✦ At the end it is interesting to see which children have paid the most attention.

39. **Hit**

✦ This is the ideal game for helping children with their multiplications – but they will never realize because it is so much fun to do!

✦ The class sit in a circle and, at the same time as counting 1, 2, 3, 4, 5 they pass a beanbag around.

✦ Whenever the number four is said or any number with four in it (14, 24, 34, 44) or multiples of the number (4, 8, 12, 16), the person who is holding the bean bag on that occasion must say 'hit'.

✦ Should one pupil miss it then they are eliminated and the whole counting process must begin again with the next person.

1..2..3..HIT..5..6..7..HIT..9..10..11..HIT..13..HIT..15..HIT..17..18..19..
HIT..21..22..23..HIT..25..26..27..HIT..29..30..31..HIT..33..HIT..35..
HIT..37..38..39..HIT..HIT..HIT..HIT..HIT..HIT..HIT..HIT..HIT..
HIT..50

40. **Guess the object**

✦ The class is divided up into three groups, each one given an object from within the room.

✦ They have ten minutes in which to think up a completely original use for the object, make up an advertisement and perform their act to the rest of the class.

✦ The most original idea, chosen by the teacher, is the winner.

41. **Whistle blow**

◆ The children stand in a circle.

◆ Whenever the teacher blows the whistle once, everyone must raise one hand in the air, if the teacher blows the whistle twice then all hands must remain down by their side.

◆ Whoever gets it wrong is eliminated from the game. To make it more frantic a third whistle and instruction could be implemented, perhaps at the third whistle everyone must stand on one leg.

42. **Reach for the sky**

✦ Knowing your right hand from your left hand can often be confusing so this is a fun way for them to remember.

✦ The players form a large circle.

✦ The teacher chooses one child to walk around the inside of the circle and when the child stops they say to whichever child is in front of them: 'Reach for the sky'.

✦ At this point the person standing in front must remain as they are, whilst the person to their right must raise their right hand and similarly the person to their left must raise their left hand.

✦ Sounds easy enough but after a while it can become challenging because whoever gets it wrong then replaces the lead role.

43. **Box of surprises**

✦ Into a large box put lots of different items from the classroom, enough for every child in the class – pencil, pen, rubber, book, crayon.

✦ Arrange the pupils in a large circle and have some music on hand. When the music begins pass the box around the circle, whenever it stops, whichever child is holding the box must close their eyes, dip their hand into the box and retrieve an object.

✦ Keeping their eyes tightly closed, just by feeling the shape and size of the item, the child has ten seconds to try to guess its identity. The teacher tells them if they are right or wrong and if correct the item is removed from the box and the game continues. If the guess is wrong, the item is returned to the box and that person must step out of the circle.

✦ The winner is the last remaining player.

44. **Mystery word**

✦ The class is formed into two teams, A and B. One pupil from team A goes to the front of the classroom and stands with their back to the whiteboard.

✦ The teacher writes a word on the whiteboard and fellow pupils have three minutes to describe the word to their team member without saying what it is. For example, 'You can use it to jump with; it's long'.

✦ If the person answers correctly the team are awarded two points. No points are awarded if they fail to answer within the time allotted or give the wrong answer. It is then the turn of team B.

✦ The winning team is the one who has the most points at the end of the game, which is when everyone has had a turn.

45. **Writing fun**

✦ The class is divided into three or four groups and each one must choose a captain.

✦ On the whiteboard, the teacher writes down a category such as fruit, clothes or animals.

✦ The aim is for each team to help their captain write down as many words as they can belonging to that category in three minutes.

✦ Afterwards the captain must stand up and reveal their list to the rest of the class.

✦ One point is awarded to each team for every word they have, two points awarded if only they have that one word and an extra point is awarded if it has been spelled correctly.

46. **Listen and answer**

✦   A super game for helping children to listen to questions being asked and respond immediately, without all the usual pauses and hesitations. Two bells or other noise makers are needed.

✦   The class is divided into two teams.

✦   Two desks and chairs are brought to the front of the classroom and from each team one member is chosen to represent their fellow players. The teacher asks them both the same question and the first one to ring their bell or make a noise, or raise their hand has the chance to answer. If they are correct they win two points for their team and continue in the game. If wrong, they must return to their team and allow another member to have a turn.

✦   The winning team is the ones to have the most points by the end of the quiz.

✦   Rules – no shouting out by fellow team members; each person has only three seconds to answer the question, otherwise they are eliminated; if someone keeps on winning points they can only remain in the seat for three attempts and then must allow another team member a try.

✦   The questions could be general ones about themselves or a random selection depending on the age of the children.

What sport do you play with a tennis racket?
What is this country called?
What doesn't shine at night in the sky?
What does shine at night in the sky?
How many letters are there in the alphabet?
When is Christmas Eve?
How do you spell … (think of a word)?
What is a baby cow called?

47. **Beanbag throw**

✦ This is a fast fun game with all children standing in a circle and the teacher in the middle holding the beanbag.

✦ The teacher throws the beanbag randomly to a child and at the same time he/she asks a question like: 'What day is it today?'

✦ The child must answer quickly and return the beanbag back to the teacher who then immediately throws it to another pupil and asks another question and the game continues.

✦ Players are only eliminated if they cannot answer the question correctly, hesitate, or drop the beanbag.

✦ Tip – for older children more difficult questions could be posed perhaps some mathematical equation, a spelling or even linked to a subject area being taught at the same time.

48. **Teacher portraits**

✦ Split the class into two teams. Draw two circles on the whiteboard and two larger ovals below to represent the outline of the torso.

✦ The teams have five minutes in which to complete a portrait of their teacher complete with eyes, nose, mouth, ears, hair, arms, legs and, if they have enough time, a designer outfit. Each child has to add something to the portrait and the winner is the team that completes within the time allocated.

✦ Warning – only to be played if the teacher has a sense of humour!

49. **Tell me the month**

✦ The teacher prepares two sets of laminated cards with 24 cards in each: the month of the year written on 12 and on the other 12 things associated with each calendar month.

✦ For example, January could be associated with snow – on one card write January and on another draw a picture of snow or a snowman. Similarly, April could be associated with Easter – on one card write April and on another card draw a picture of some Easter eggs.

✦ Divide the children into two teams. Sit the groups on the floor and give each one a set of cards. Allow a few minutes to match the months up with the pictures.

✦ Tip – you don't need to concentrate on themes for each month just in general what children associate with them.

50. **Memory**

✦ This is the ideal game for children who are confident with the alphabet. Arrange the children in two lines so that everyone is facing the same direction.

✦ Provide the last student in each line with an alphabet card. The idea is that they must write whatever letter they are holding on the back of the person in front of them using their finger.

✦ It is then the turn of the second person to do the same with the next child's back and so it continues along the line until it reaches the first child in the line who must then call out what the letter is.

✦ If they guess correctly they are awarded one point for their team and the child at the front of the line must go to the back. Another game can continue. Children can only move back if they have successfully guessed the identity of the letter otherwise they must remain where they are.

52

51. **Remember, remember**

✦ Depending on the age/size of class you may well need to recruit the help of a classroom assistant to ensure there is no cheating in this game. To demonstrate how to play choose several children and get the rest of the class to watch.

✦ Lay a pack of ordinary playing cards randomly out on the table face up. The children have 60 seconds in which to study them before turning them over.

✦ Each child now takes it in turn to point to a card and say what they think it is, before turning it over for everyone to see. If they have guessed correctly they can retain the card and have another turn. If they are incorrect the card is then replaced face down and it is the turn of the next player.

✦ The winner is the one who has the most cards at the end of the game.

✦ Tip – You can use more or less cards depending on the age of the children.

Talking Games

Studies have shown that poor oracy (talking and listening) skills, limit progress in reading and writing. The fun activities in this chapter will help them to practise these vital skills in fun and enjoyable ways.

Some activities, such as *Clap, clap* (Activity 59) and *Potato, potato, potato* (Activity 69) focus on listening and attention skills, encouraging pupils to attend to and concentrate on sounds.

Others focus more on understanding and expressive language. For example, in *Animals and birds* (Activity 58), the children need to quickly give examples of either an animal or bird and in *Going home* (Activity 60) the children will need to concentrate to be sure they don't miss a statement that relates to them.

Telling stories is always popular and pupils will enjoy *Tell me a story* (Activity 62) and *Once upon a time* (Activity 63), whereas *Theatre time* (Activity 65) will help to develop their drama skills.

53. **Yes or no**

✦ The three main elements of this game include: listening to the question being asked, thinking about the answer and making a decision, which the child feels confident enough in seeing through. It is a game for all ages and abilities.

✦ The teacher lays a piece of coloured tape on the floor (or if carpeted use a length of string/row of rulers). One side of the line is designated Yes and the other side is No.

✦ The class are then asked various questions, either based on a subject they have studied in class: spellings, multiplication, or on general topics; the answer can only be yes or no. When the question is posed whoever thinks the answer is true must stand on the Yes side of the tape and for those who think the answer is wrong must stand on the No side of the tape.

✦ When the correct answer is revealed then whoever is standing on the wrong side of the tape must sit down until the game is over. The winner is the last person who is standing.

54. **Dong, ding-a-ling**

✦ In this game one child comes to the front of the classroom where the teacher gives them a category, ie something we use in the home. The player has several seconds to think of an item and then whisper its identity to the teacher. They have three minutes to try and demonstrate their secret object to the rest of the class using no words only actions.

✦ The fun begins when the demonstration is over and the children try guessing what the object could be. In return the player can only answer "dong" when the guess called out is wrong and "ding-a-ling" when the guess is correct, at which time whoever guessed correctly can have a turn.

55. **Silence**

✦ This is a fun game, especially for the teacher, because the object is that no one must speak.

✦ There is very little preparatory work other than numbering pieces of card according to the number of children in the classroom, eg 1, 2, 3, 4, 5.

✦ Each of those cards are then laminated and placed on the floor. The children are then given three minutes to each pick up a number and stand in that sequence according to the ones they have chosen but the secret is to do this without talking.

✦ Other ideas which could be used include standing in order of height, letters of the alphabet, the children could write their own house/telephone numbers on laminated cards and arrange them in numerical order, older children could re-arrange clock faces in order of the times shown or arrange historical events in chronological order.

56. **Catch it if you can**

✦ Everyone sits together in a circle. The teacher gives a child a beanbag. That child must, before throwing it to another class member, say their name and then something about themselves, ie 'Peter, I like playing football'.

✦ Whoever is in receipt of the beanbag must then say, 'Peter likes playing football. Anna, I like reading', before passing it to another class member who must now remember what the two previous people said before adding their own.

✦ The game continues until the children begin to forget what the previous callers had said, at which point they are out of the game and a new game can begin.

57. **Dancing beats**

✦ This isn't so much a game as something the children will enjoy doing for fifteen minutes or so. The teacher chants a simple mantra, ie rum, rum, ra, ra and in doing so makes a different movement each time.

✦ For example:
Rum (click fingers)
Rum (click fingers)
Ra (clap hands)
Ra (clap hands)

✦ The children then have to repeat the mantra together with the movement. At the beginning do so very very slowly and then gradually make it faster and faster until some children will be clapping their hands instead of clicking their fingers and vice versa, but they will have a lot of fun. To announce the game is over shout 'over'.

58. **Animals and birds**

✦ The children all sit in a semi-circle facing the teacher who randomly points to a pupil and says animal, bird or fish. Within three seconds whoever the teacher pointed at must name something from within that category.

✦ For example:
Teacher says: 'Fish'
Student says: 'Haddock'
Teacher says: 'Bird'
Student replies: 'Sparrow'.

✦ The game continues until one child gets confused and names a bird when it should have been an animal, or can't remember anything within that category or announces one that has previously been mentioned. That person is then eliminated from the game.

59. **Clap, clap**

✦ Everyone forms a circle with the teacher standing in the middle. The teacher begins counting: 1, 2, 3, 4, 5. At the call of 3, everyone must clap their hands.

✦ To make the game more exciting the teacher might count slowly or even clap her hands at the wrong time and whoever copies is immediately out of the game. Watch out for the excited children who clap before the number is said (there will be plenty of those).

60. **Going home**

✦ The whole class form a circle and stand with a chair in front of them. The aim is for everyone to get around the circle and back to his or her own chair in the fastest time possible. This is done simply by answering correctly the questions asked by the teacher.

✦ The teacher makes statements such as: 'You have a pet at home', 'You have a brother', 'You like playing football'. Every time a child answers 'Yes' they then move one chair to their right. If the statement doesn't apply to them they stay where they are. Don't worry if at times queues are forming and it seems that no one is moving; this just makes the game more exciting.

✦ The first one home back to their chair is the winner.

61. **Odd things out**

✦ Some preliminary work is required by the teacher for this game to work successfully.

✦ Enrol the help of a classroom assistant to take the children out into the corridor for several minutes whilst you change several things around in the classroom.

✦ For example: put the wastebasket on a table, the teacher's chair at a pupil's desk, put up/remove something from the classroom wall. Make as many changes as you can within three minutes, then allow the children back in and arrange them into pairs. The aim is to find as many wrongly placed things in the classroom as they can. The pair who find the most things win.

✦ Tip – some ideas: remove a picture from the wall, put someone's chair on their desk, put a teacher's chair at a pupil's desk, line some rulers on the windowsill edge, stand a pot of pencils upside down, put a piece of cloth over the clock, write backwards on the whiteboard.

62. **Tell me a story**

✦   Children love to tell stories and they will enjoy this game. Divide the class into small groups of five or six and have them sit across from one another.

✦   The first team player in team A relates the first sentence of a story (it can be about anything) and when they stop the opposing first member of the other team immediately takes up the story adding their own sentence. It is then the turn of number two in team A, who must then add on another sentence, trying to keep to the same theme before number two in team B adds their own sentence.

✦   An example:
Team A (Player 1) – Trigger was a brown horse who
Team B (Player 1) – loved to play in the farmer's field with the other horses
Team A (Player 2) – but he was getting so old
Team B – (Player 2) that sometimes he would run off into another field

✦   It's just a fun but challenging game to play, with no winners or losers, and for the teacher it is interesting to see which team manages to keep up with their story.

The big pink...............

penguin decided to........

fly to Hawaii.........

wearing a...............

63. **Once upon a time ...**

✦ Children love story time and they will enjoy this game because they make their very own classroom story up with each child playing a role.

✦ Everyone sits around in a circle and the teacher starts by giving one word. The children take it in turns to contribute one word. The only criteria is that the word chosen must make sense in the context of the earlier words.

✦ As an example:
Boxer, loved, his, walks, in, the, morning. A different pupil contributed each word written in italics. A player can decide to end a sentence and begin a new one. The game continues until a story has evolved.

64. **What's my job?**

✦ The teacher chooses one pupil and tells them to act out a job. The remainder of the class must try to guess the occupation. In order to do so, each child is allowed to ask one question that could help to find out what that job is, but the player can only reply yes or no.

✦ Whoever guesses correctly is the winner and they have a turn.

65. Theatre time

✦ Children love reciting nursery rhymes and being entertained, so why not turn a wet playtime into a fun playtime and get children to make up their own small theatre.

✦ Choose a popular children's nursery rhyme such as Hey Diddle Diddle, Jack and Jill, or Little Bo Beep, and as the children recite it, write it down on the whiteboard.

✦ The teacher should then select a number of pupils to re-enact the nursery rhyme in front of their fellow classmates but it doesn't necessarily mean that only two pupils can participate. The exciting thing is that as many people as you want can be involved.

✦ For example:

Jack and Jill
Went up the hill
To fetch a pail of water
Jack fell down and broke his crown
And Jill came running after … .

✦ As a class you could spend some time discussing the different people that could be involved in the story: Jack and Jill, then what about the hill, think about the sheep or cows that may have been grazing. There may have been other people walking around the area, mothers out with their young children, or dogs running around. Then as Jack came back down again there could be an ambulance coming to help them, other people hurrying over, or even a doctor. What about a reporter and photographer who may have witnessed the accident?

✦ By the end of the discussion everyone in the class could have a role to play. Acting it out is so much fun and think how educational too.

66. **Keeping mum**

✦ If there is one thing children find difficult to do, it is to keep quiet for any length of time, even a few minutes. However, on this occasion the reason for remaining silent, is the point of the game.

✦ The teacher uses an egg timer, which is placed on their desk, and when it begins everyone has to keep their mouths firmly closed and stay perfectly still; anyone who makes the slightest noise is eliminated, even if they shuffle around in their seat.

✦ Those who flinch or make any unnecessary noise or movement are eliminated. The game continues until there is only one child remaining. Children love this game because they like to prove to teacher that they can remain quiet.

67. **Shine, shine**

✦ Everyone stands in a circle and the teacher calls out a word.

✦ The first person must say the first letter of that word, the second person calls out the second letter, the third person the third letter and so on until the word is spelled out. Should a word be misspelled then the person to say the wrong letter must sit down at their desk and the game continues. However, when the last letter of the word is reached the person who says it must then turn to the next person and say 'shine' as it is at this point whoever has been shined must return to their seat.

✦ Once a player has been shined, the teacher calls out another word and the game continues until only one player is remaining.

68. **What's missing**

✦ All the children sit around in a circle and the teacher places twelve different things on a tray that can be found in the classroom, ie pencil, pen, rubber, ruler, book, crayon.

✦ After the children have looked at the tray for several minutes the teacher then takes it over to their desk and removes something and gives the rest of the items a quick shuffle, before replacing the tray in the middle of the group.

✦ Whoever correctly identifies whichever item was removed from the tray takes the next turn to remove an object for the rest of the class to have a guess.

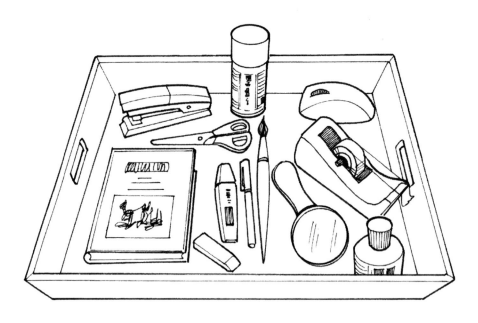

69. **Potato, potato, potato**

✦ Concentration and fun are the main elements of this game in which the children sit in a circle and each child is given the name of a vegetable.

✦ One pupil, chosen by the teacher, has to stand in the middle of the circle and call out the name of a vegetable three times, eg potato, potato, potato.

✦ Whoever has been given the *potato* name must butt in by calling out *potato* before the other person has managed to say it the three times.

✦ If they do so successfully, the person in the middle must choose another vegetable but if they are not quick enough they replace the person in the middle.

70. **Holiday time**

✦ This game is loosely based on the familiar 'I went to the market' but in this instance it is 'I went on my holidays'.

✦ The players sit together in a circle and each child has to think of one item they will take with them in their suitcase, ie 'I took my swimming costume in my case', and then the next player must repeat those words and then add something different of their own.

✦ Every player has a turn at adding something else to the suitcase but they must also recall whatever other items their previous friends mentioned and if they forget they are out of the game. Whoever remembers the most items is the winner.

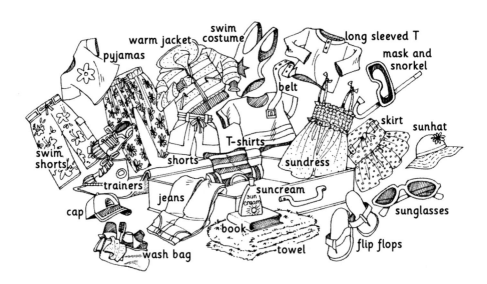

71. **Talking is good**

✦ Bring in two old telephones if you have them, or be imaginative and the children can make their own in an art class with cardboard boxes and other recycled materials.

✦ Divide the class into two teams and explain that the object of the game is for each player within the team to have one minute to hold a telephone conversation with an imaginary friend. They must not pause, hesitate or repeat anything. When their minute is up they have to hand the phone to the next player of their team.

✦ If they are able to sustain the conversation they are awarded a point. The team to have the most points at the end of the game is the winner.

72. **What word?**

✦ The teacher chooses someone to stand with his/her back to the whiteboard.

✦ Whilst the pupil faces the rest of the class the teacher writes down a word or perhaps a phrase on the whiteboard. The rest of the class then have to explain what is meant by this so the pupil standing in front of them can guess what has been written.

✦ Whoever gives the best explanation enabling the pupil to guess correctly can then take a turn.

73. **Do as you are told**

✦ Some preparation work is required before playing this game. The teacher should write a number of adjectives on pieces of card, eg slow, lively, scary.

✦ On the whiteboard they should write an activity, eg 'brush your hair', the teacher then chooses a pupil who comes to the front of the class and the teacher shows them a card with an adjective written on, eg lively. The pupil then has to carry out the task written on the board in the way described by the adjective.If the adjective is lively the pupil must brush their hair in a lively way.

✦ But the fun part begins when the rest of the class have to guess what that adjective could be. The one who answers correctly then has a turn at the next action.

✦ Tip – for younger children it might be advisable for the teacher to write down on the board the adjectives that are found written on the cards.

74. **Walk around**

✦   This is a fun game, which requires all the classroom furniture to be put to one side for a while. It could be played equally well in the hall.

✦   The teacher plays some music and whenever the music stops they call out a number, up to as many pupils as there is in the class. Whatever number is called the children must form themselves into that number group. Those who fail are eliminated from that round.

✦   To make it more exciting don't forget to randomly call out number one.

✦   The game continues until there is only one person remaining.

75. **Racing transport**

✦ This game may be more suited to playing in the hall.

✦ Sit the children in a row facing the front of the room. At the front of the class place two chairs alongside one another approximately a meter apart but make sure there is plenty of room around them. Select two children to sit on the chairs. The object of the game is to see who imitates the mode of transport best.

✦ Sounds fun and it is, especially when the teacher tells them to behave like a motorcycle, or fly like an aeroplane together with accompanying sounds. After the count of three, each child must get up from their seat and quickly go over to the other chair in the action of the chosen transport.

✦ The rest of the class have to judge whom, in their opinion, was the best and the most realistic. At the end of the game, when everyone has had a turn the winners play against one another and the ultimate winner is chosen by the class.

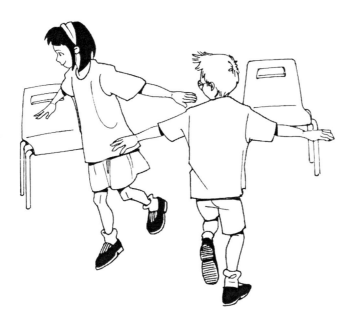

76. I like

✦ Sit the children in a circle and select one child to begin the game by saying 'I like playing football'. Continue round the circle with each child saying what they like.

✦ To make it even more exciting they could add on what the previous child had said they liked, eg 'I like ice-cream, he likes playing football'.

77. May I?

◆ This is guaranteed to be a popular classroom game for all ages. The teacher will need to think of a selection of questions to ask appropriate to the age group.

◆ Measure out ten rows of sticky coloured tape on the floor approximately one adult footstep from one another. Then have the children line up alongside one another behind the first line.

◆ Ask one child a question at a time, ie 'What does a horse say?' and if that child answers correctly they can then move onto the next line. If however, they don't get it correct they must stay where they are.

◆ The winner is the first child to reach the final line first.

78. **Sixty seconds**

✦ To play this game an egg timer is required.

✦ Organize the children to sit in a circle. Set the timer and then hand it over to a child. Ask them a question and immediately they answer it, tell them to pass the timer to the next pupil who has to answer the same question and pass the egg timer on to the next child.

✦ Whoever is left holding the egg timer when it goes off is out of the game.

✦ Set the timer again and ask a different question. Younger children might like to count or even recite letters of the alphabet.

Word Games

Playing with words is an ideal way to help children to develop their language skills, giving them the confidence to manipulate language and feel in control of it.

Alphabet split (Activity 103) is ideal for use with younger children, to help them to recognize the letters of the alphabet. Others, such as *Spelling contest* (Activity 80) are more suited to older children. However, most can be adapted to suit a wide range of ages and abilities.

The ability to play with words is an important skill to develop in all languages. Some activities, such as *Gone hunting* (Activity 88) and *Bonjour* (Activity 93) link specifically to teaching a foreign language and many of the others can be adapted for this purpose.

79. **Word search**

✦ Children of all ages love playing word searches and although there are lots of resources for teachers to download off the Internet it is well worth the time to make up some of your own classroom ones.

✦ Each child could say a word that will form the whole class word search and if the teacher draws a large grid on the whiteboard, then each child can take turns to add their words. As you progress it will get harder and harder to fit all the words in.

80. **Spelling contest**

✦ The teacher divides the class into two teams and asks one person from the first team to spell a word. As they spell it out the teacher writes the word on the whiteboard. If they get it correct, their team is awarded a point and then the opposing team take a turn.

✦ The game continues until each team member has been given a word to spell. The winners are those who have the most points at the end of the game.

apple
A P P L E

81. **Can you remember?**

✦ This is a good game to play in teams and involves all the children sitting around in a circle. The teacher places a selection of card pairs spread faced down randomly in a grid on the floor in front of them. The teacher then asks a child a question and if they answer correctly they may turn over two cards.

✦ Should those two cards match (eg, two 4s) then the pupil can keep them but if the cards don't match (perhaps one is a number 3 and the other 7) then those cards must be replaced back into the pack face down again.

✦ The trick is that the children should try to remember the sequence in which the cards are replaced and so know where they are. To make the game easier, the teacher could design a pack of cards with fruit/vegetables.

✦ Tip – The older and more confident the children get, the more cards you can use.

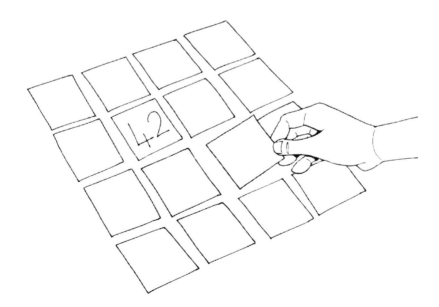

82. **Wastepaper ball**

✦ All the children will love to play this game and it is so simple. Basically the wastepaper bin becomes the target; you can either use some crumpled up paper formed into a round ball or alternatively, a soft spongy ball.

✦ The class is divided up into two teams. Sit the teams in lines, one behind another on the floor.

✦ Meanwhile the wastepaper bin is located at the front of the class and the teacher calls a child from each team in turn to answer a question; it could be a spelling or a generally based question. If they answer correctly they are awarded one point for their team.

✦ The fun part is next. The child stands a distance away from the wastepaper bin and tries to score an extra point by netting the ball in the bin.

✦ If the answer is wrong the child does not get the chance to try throwing the ball into the bin.

✦ The winning team is the one to have been awarded the most points at the end of the game.

83. Backwards, forwards

✦ This is an interesting game that the teacher will have lots of fun creating. Some preliminary work will have to be done which involves the teacher writing down some sentences (or for younger children, words) backwards.

✦ Divide the class into teams or they can work on their own tables. The teacher writes one word/phrase backwards on the board and each table has one minute to try and work out what that word/phrase is. If they are correct they win one point and it is the turn of the next table.

✦ The winning table is the one to have unscrambled the most words at the end of a ten-minute game.

84. Puzzling time

✦ Some preparation work is necessary for this game. Laminate old pictures (eg, from an old catalogue) and cut each picture into six pieces. Make sufficient so that each pupil has one puzzle piece. Give them five minutes in which to look around the classroom at other pupils' pieces and join up the correct puzzles.

✦ The group which is the fastest wins the game.

85. Give it time

✦ Separate the class into two teams. One person elected from team A has to come up to the front of class where the teacher hands them a piece of paper which has three action words written on it such as: jump, sleep, hop. The selected person then mimes the actions.

✦ In three minutes fellow team members have to guess as many of the actions written on the paper as they can, with one point awarded for each correct answer. It is then the turn of the opposing team.

✦ Play three rounds with a different player from each team coming to the front each time. Whichever team gets the most points at the end of the game is the winner.

86. Hunt the letter

✦ This game can either be played in small groups or individually. Each pupil/group is given a letter of the alphabet and within a set time, perhaps five minutes, the pupils have to find as many classroom items as they are able to beginning with that allocated letter.

✦ Perhaps one group was given the letter 'R' in which case they would look for any objects in the classroom beginning with that letter and write them down on a sheet of paper, eg rubber, ruler and rug.

✦ The winner is the team who finds the most things and writes them down within the set time.

87. **Up, down, across, stop**

✦ With this game the children can either play in their respective class groups or be divided up into teams.

✦ The teacher writes one word on the whiteboard together with lots of definitions dotted about the board, only one of which is true.

✦ The groups then have one minute to quietly discuss amongst themselves which they think is the true definition of that word. One person is then chosen to go to the front of the class and become the pointer. They are blindfolded.

✦ One by one each player must call out an instruction to his or her team member on how to reach the right definition. This can only be done by one-word explanations like: left, right, down, up. Following on after each instruction the caller must say stop. When the correct definition is reached they must shout out 'Got it'.

✦ To make the game more exciting there are certain rules to follow: only one person at a time may give an instruction and the group must take it in turns to call out instructions.

✦ No one can help another player and there must be no calling out. The pointer must simply do as they are told and when the definition is arrived at the team must shout 'Got it' and the game is over.

✦ Continue until all the teams have chosen what they believe to be the correct definition. The teacher can then show the correct definition. To start the next round the word and the correct definition can be rubbed off and replaced with a different one.

88. **Gone hunting**

✦ This is great fun for older children who are learning a foreign language, perhaps French.

✦ On the whiteboard draw up a list in French of eight to ten common items found in the classroom, eg un stylo (pen), un livre (book), une règle (ruler), un crayon (pencil) and arrange the children into groups of five. Sitting in their groups they have to translate into English as many of those words as they can. After ten minutes they have five more minutes to try to find as many of these objects as they can.

✦ When the time is up, the group with the most items on their desk are the winners.

✦ A variation would be for the words to be written in English, and for the children to translate as many of the words as they can into the French equivalent.

89. **Reach for the circles**

✦ Children of all ages will love playing this game and it can be made more difficult for the older ones, eg by saying the numbers in a foreign language.

✦ On the whiteboard draw a huge circle and inside draw lots of smaller circles each with a number on from 1–20. Divide the class into two teams.

✦ Standing several meters away from the whiteboard each child has to say which number they are going to try to hit and then throw a small soft ball at the number. If they hit it they earn whatever point was on that circle.

✦ The winning team is the one to have scored the most points by the end of the game, but they must keep their own scores.

90. Buttoned up

✦ Bring two men's shirts into class and divide the class up into two teams. Make sure that each shirt has the same number of buttons.

✦ At the word go one person on each team puts the shirt on and begins to fasten the buttons down the front. The one who is buttoned up first is then asked a question by the teacher and if they get that question correct they are awarded one point, but if the answer is wrong or they don't know it then the opposing team member gets a chance to answer.

✦ The next round begins with the next player from each team going through the same procedure.

91. Talk about it

✦ Children love talking and this is a game which they will really enjoy playing. Divide the pupils into groups. Choose one pupil from the first group and give them fifteen seconds to talk about a chosen subject without pausing, hesitating or repeating words. If they are able to do this they are awarded one point for their team. The teacher then chooses another pupil from the opposing team to have a turn.

✦ The winning team are those awarded the most points at the end of the game.

✦ You could choose a topic related to your work in other subjects, eg Evaporation or Henry VIII.

92. **Secret word**

✦ This is a super game played in pairs. The object is for one person to find out the mystery word their opponent has written down on the paper.

✦ Each person writes down a word on a piece of paper containing at least five letters (more if the children are older) and the only clue they are able to offer their opponent is to identify the category it is taken from.

✦ Player one lets his opponent know the subject area/category his 'secret' word belongs in.

✦ The second player will then take a guess at player one's secret word.

✦ Player one must then tell player two if any letters are common in both words, for example if the secret word was 'daisy' and player two had said 'tulip' then player one would say that there was one letter that was in both words, whereas if they had said 'pansy', player one would say three letters the same.

✦ The game continues until the guesser gives up or solves the word in which case it is the turn of the other person.

93. Bonjour

✦ Children will enjoy playing this game, whatever stage of learning a foreign language they have reached.

✦ All you require is a soft toy that can be easily hidden. Give it a French name, perhaps Jacques (or an appropriate name to the language being taught).

✦ The teacher chooses a pupil who is then asked to leave the room. Whilst they are out the toy is given to another child in the class who should hide the toy in their desk or on their lap so that the other child cannot see it.

✦ The player then enters the classroom and they have to try and locate the soft toy by asking any of their classmates but they *must* ask the question in French, eg 'Bonjour, Je m'appelle (child's name), et toi?'

✦ In reply the pupil should say, 'Bonjour, Je m'appelle (their name)', and only if they have the hidden toy reply: 'Je m'appelle (and the name of the toy)'.

✦ The guesser has only limited chances after which time the teacher then asks 'Ou est (name of the toy)?'. To make the finding slightly easier you could provide the guesser with a basic idea whereabouts in the room the soft toy is hidden. Then whoever has the toy takes their turn at leaving the classroom.

✦ If two or three children are involved in asking the question, it becomes a race. Great fun!

✦ Tip – it is important that the children know the name of the toy in French.

94. I say, I say

✦ Have the children sit around in a circle and prepare some Post-it® notes or 'stickies', each with a different animal written on it. Stick one on the forehead of each child.

✦ Choose a child to start the game. The chosen child can ask the person sitting on their right three questions, to which the answer can only be yes or no, in order to find out their own identity.

> For example:
> Do I have four legs?
> Do I have a tail?
> Do I bark?

✦ If, after asking three questions, the person fails to guess their own identity they remain with the 'stickie' on. It is then the turn of the person sitting on their right. The game continues until there is only one person remaining with a 'stickie' on and they are the loser.

✦ If a child guesses their identity they can remove their 'stickies' but still be asked questions.

✦ Tip – older children might like to try this game using nouns or certain jobs.

95. **Slam**

✦ This is a fun game in which the teacher thinks up some questions, perhaps mathematical equations, and writes the answers randomly down on the whiteboard.

✦ The class is divided into two teams and the first player from each team has to come to the front of the classroom and stand either side of the whiteboard.

✦ When the teacher asks the question the first person to point to the correct answer is awarded three points for their team and whoever lost must return to their own team and choose another player to come to the front of the class and pit their wits against the winner.

✦ Whoever answers the question correctly remains at the front of the class trying to win points for their team but after three correct answers they must return to their team so another player can come forward.

✦ The winning team is the one who has the most points at the end of the game.

96. **Bow wow wow**

✦ One pupil plays the part of the dog and sits in a chair with their back to the class.

✦ A short ruler is placed on the floor underneath the chair (this is to represent the bone).

✦ Whilst the dog is sitting with his/her eyes closed (or blindfolded) someone creeps up and takes the bone and then hides it somewhere upon themselves.

✦ When the person returns to their seat the whole class, ask: 'One of us has stolen your bone can you find its new home?' At which point the dog then has three chances to guess who the thief might be. If they are wrong, then whoever stole the bone becomes the dog.

✦ If they guessed correctly then the dog stays for another game.

97. **Baker, Baker**

✦ Everyone sits around in a circle apart from one person, chosen by the teacher, who has to sit in the middle.

✦ This person must close their eyes and the remainder of the class say: 'Baker, Baker, bake us some bread, for none of my children have been fed.'

✦ Whilst the children are reciting this they pass around an object behind their backs to one another, perhaps a small box or a glove.

✦ The baker then has to reply: 'bring me some flour and it will be done, two large loaves and some buns.'

✦ At the final word the passing of the object must stop and whoever has it must make sure it is hidden behind their back.

✦ The baker can then open their eyes and, just by looking at the faces of the players, has 20 seconds to try to guess who has his 'flour'. If he fails, he changes place with whoever was holding the 'flour'.

98. Spot the difference

✦ Divide the class into two teams: team A and team B.

✦ Team A looks at their opposing team members for two minutes and makes a mental note of everything about them; they then leave the classroom for a few minutes.

✦ Whilst out of the classroom each members of team B changes one thing about themselves, it could be putting a jumper on back to front, putting a pencil in their pocket, undoing a shoelace.

✦ After three minutes team A return to the room and each member has to guess any differences they can spot in the opposing team members. One point is awarded for each correct answer.

99. Tell us a story

✦ This entertaining game isn't just for wet playtimes; it could equally be integrated into a class lesson.

✦ Divide the class into groups of four or five and give them each a picture taken out of a magazine such as a beach scene, a certain animal or a group of children playing together. Whatever the picture is, the group have ten minutes to think up a story of their own relating to that picture.

100. Who am I?

✦ Write the names of famous characters from history, items of furniture, (or for younger children nursery rhyme characters) on pieces of paper, enough for every child in the class, and stick them onto their backs. The aim is for the children to find out their identity by asking other classmates question. In turn heir classmates can only answer yes or no.

✦ For example:
Question: Do I sit at it?
Answer: Yes
Question: Do I have four legs?
Answer: Yes
Question: Am I a table?
Answer: Yes

✦ Only then can they remove the sticky label and sit down. The game continues until everyone has found out their identity but be vigilant there is no cheating going on.

101. Have a giggle

✦   This is truly a game to play in the hall but is so infectious it is guaranteed that the children will want to play it time and time again.

✦   The object is for each child to lie on the floor in a zigzag format so that each child lies with their head gently resting on the stomach of the next one.

✦   Whoever is at the start of the line has to call 'Ha' and the child whose head is on their stomach must then follow on and call 'Ha' and so the game continues with each child adding a 'Ha' and soon everyone is laughing.

✦   Tip – as an alternative you could replace the 'Ha' with a number or go through the letters of the alphabet.

102. What is the animal?

✦ Prepare a selection of flashcards with farm/wild animals on and place them in an envelope.

✦ Ask the children to sit in a circle while you put on some music Give the children a softball or beanbag to pass around the circle as the music plays. Whenever the music stops, whoever has the beanbag must go to the teacher who will secretly reveal to them a card depicting an animal.

✦ That child must then go into the middle of the circle and act out what the animal is in any way they choose. The rest of the class has to try to guess the identity.

✦ It doesn't matter if no one can guess. After a few minutes simply replace that picture and round two can begin.

103. Alphabet split

✦ This super game for young children will help them with their alphabet and also encourage them to work together with their peers.

✦ Draw, cut out and laminate the letters of the alphabet and colour each letter differently.

✦ Cut up each letter into several smaller pieces and hand them out to the children.

✦ The idea is for the teacher to call out the letters in alphabetic order and whoever is holding any part of that letter must go up to the teacher and help put that letter together.

104. **Pin the tail**

✦ This is an old party game but never fails to entertain children.

✦ Laminate the picture of a horse or donkey and attach it to the whiteboard, but make sure it is bereft of some part of its anatomy, perhaps an ear or its tail.

✦ The class can either be separated into teams or play individually but the aim is for them to come up to the whiteboard (one by one) where they will be blindfolded.

✦ Give them a gentle turn around and then armed with the missing piece with some Blutac® on the back, they have to try to pinpoint wherever the tail or ear should be on the animal.

✦ It's just a lot of fun but can be made educational to help young children learn to identify different parts of the animal.

Computer games

There is a great deal of controversy surrounding the role computer games play in schools. Some parents strongly object to them, feeling that children should use their brains more than relying on technology to answer questions; whilst in the opposing corner, researchers and many experts believe that computer games should be part of the school curriculum and do play a large integral part of a child's educational development. Whoever is right or wrong research studies have shown:

✦	Some games can offer children a great deal of things which conventional teaching cannot.

✦	It has been proven that unmotivated children very often get fired up when provided with information in a different format.

✦	Games can be an effective way of reaching those children who haven't responded to conventional teaching methods.

✦	Computer games have proven to encourage gifted children to apply critical thinking, problem solving and other higher level skills to subjects they already know.

✦	Many games have led to stealth education whereby all children have such a good time that they don't even realize they are learning.

Gaming websites for children

There are literally thousands of websites that contain computer games for children and it is always advisable for teachers to look at the respective sites before allowing the children access. Here below are selections that have been chosen for primary school aged children.

http://www.ictgames.com/resources.html
Numeracy games

http://www.bbc.co.uk/cbeebies
http://www.bbc.co.uk/cbbc
BBC – all subjects

http://www.show.me.uk/games/games.html
Here you will find a range of different games suited to many curriculum topics, such a science, history and art.

http://www.teachingtime.co.uk/ – great site for maths and helping children learning to tell the time.

http://www.funbrain.com/ – some great games for across the ages but beware that it is American

http://www.teachingandlearningresources.co.uk/sitemap.shtml – this is a good website that links on to other websites for games.

Index

Other 100+ titles available from Brilliant Publications.

A wonderful collection of traditional and new outdoor games aimed at KS1 and KS2 pupils that will soon become playground favourites.

Activities will suit individual pupils, groups or even the whole class.

Uses readily available equipment such as balls and skipping ropes.

100+ Fun Ideas for Practicing Modern Foreign Languages

137 tried and tested activities which can be used to develop oracy and literacy skills in any language.

Enjoyable, interactive activities that are guaranteed to get an enthusiastic response from all pupils.

Covers most of the oracy and literacy objectives in the KS2 Framework for languages.

100+ FUN IDEAS Practising Modern Foreign Languages in the Primary Classroom

Activities for Developing Oracy and Literacy Skills

Sue Cave · Brilliant Publications

Perform to an audience

38. Puppet story-telling

- Puppets give older children an opportunity to retell a story or rhyme which they have been reading in class. This could be, for example, a familiar fairy tale recounted in the target language.

- Appropriately dressed puppets could be used to act it out and retell it.

- You could ask older children in Key Stage 2 to perform the story or rhyme to the younger children or parents in a class assembly.

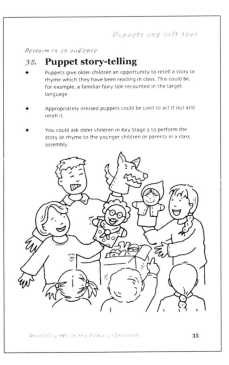

Oracy
O3.2, O3.3, O3.4, O4.4

These games with balls, bean bags and dice encourage children to listen for particular sounds, words and phrases, as well as to respond to them, perform simple communicative tasks and respond to questions.

Practising language using single words or phrases

56. Add up the dice

- If your school's resource cupboard has enough dice to give small teams of children two or three dice each, you could play a simple elimination game.

- Ask the children to roll the dice and add up the numbers.

- Each team tells the rest what their total is and the team with the lowest number goes out. The game continues until only one group remains.

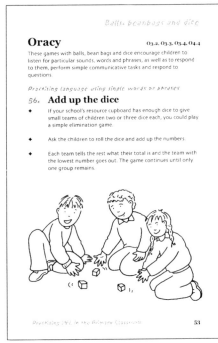

100+ Fun Ideas for Art Activites

Easy to prepare and enjoyable activities that children will love.

The activites in this book introduce a wide range of art skills and media, and are compatible with the National Curriculum. Activities are suitable for use both in the classroom, at home or in children's clubs. Although primarily aimed at 7–11 year olds, most of the activities can be adapted for younger children.

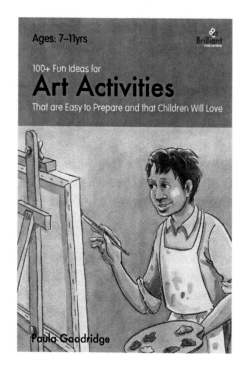

Ages: 7–11yrs

Brilliant
PUBLICATIONS

100+ Fun Ideas for

Art Activities

That are Easy to Prepare and that Children Will Love

Paula Goodridge

Printing

Activity C
You will need: plastic sheet or Perspex sheets; printing ink in a variety of colours; rollers; paper; pencils.

◆ You can repeat either of the previous activities, but this time try using more colours. Simply roller part of the plastic sheet or Perspex with one coloured ink and then another part with a different colour, before making any marks. Place the paper on the ink and follow instructions from either Activity A or B.

80

Art Activities

Textiles

63. **Christmas stockings**
You will need: pencils; felt; stocking stencil; PVA glue or needles and thread; sequins; ribbons and buttons.

◆ Give each child a simple stocking stencil and ask them to cut out two stocking shapes in felt of their choice.

◆ Cut a piece of ribbon to make a loop. This will attach the stocking to your tree!

◆ Glue or sew the felt pieces together, inserting the ribbon loop, so that it is firmly attached.

◆ You could decorate your stockings with sequins, ribbons or buttons.

64. **Glove puppets**
You will need: felt; glove puppet stencil (see page 124); glue or needles and threads; wool; buttons; scraps of fabrics.

◆ Prepare a stencil of your hand to make a glove puppet. (You could use the stencil on page 124, enlarged if necessary.)

◆ Use the stencil to cut two glove puppet shapes from felt.

◆ Stick or sew these together, leaving the bottom open for your hand.

◆ Decorate each puppet as you wish, using wool for hair and buttons for eyes.

◆ Children will love making up scripts for a puppet play afterwards, so this is a great link to play writing in literacy. They could perform to the infants!

62

Art Activities

Wet Playtimes

100+ Fun Ideas for Science Investigations

This book contains exciting, fun classroom experiments to help teach scientific investigation.

The activities require a minimum of preparation and only the simplest of science equipment. Each activity provides opportunities for children to develop their skills of scientific enquiry.

The easy-to-use layout, closely matches the statutory and non-statutory guidelines and schemes of work for Key Stages 1 and 2, and will make this an invaluable book for all primary teachers.

Ages: 5–11yrs — Brilliant

100+ Fun Ideas for
Science Investigation
In the Primary Classroom

Anita Loughrey

Life Processes and Living Things (KS1)

5. Does the tallest person have the biggest feet?

You will need: tape measures and rulers; chalk; a copy of the chart for each pair; shoe size information.

♦ As a homework task, ask the children to find out their shoe size.

♦ Fill in the chart.

Name	Shoe size	Height

♦ In pairs, the children should measure how tall they are by standing against a wall with their feet flat on the floor and marking their height with chalk.

♦ Encourage the children to use standard measures such as tape measures to calculate their height. Less able children may need adult support. For comparisons to be made, the same units need to be used.

♦ Explain that the smaller feet will be sizes 10, 11, 12 and 13, whereas the larger feet will be sizes 1 and 2 etc.

More ideas:
♦ Who is the tallest in the class?

♦ Who has the largest feet in the class?

♦ Are they the same person?

Science Investigations — 11

Ages 9–11   Living Things in their Environments

40. Which seeds have the most effective parachutes?

What you need: seeds and fruit with parachutes or wings, eg. dandelions, sycamore and ash seeds; tweezers; magnifying glasses; container to keep the seeds in whilst not in use.

♦ Predict which seed has the best parachute.

♦ This experiment is better conducted indoors, as the wind can have an adverse effect on the results.

♦ Working in pairs, the children should have races with the different seeds to see which falls the fastest and which falls the slowest.

♦ Use tweezers to lift the seeds so as not to damage their parachutes or wings.

♦ Explain to the class that the slower they fall, the better the parachute. The parachutes are meant to help disperse the seeds, and a seed's weight helps determine the type of parachute (downy parachutes for tiny seeds, propellers for heavier seeds etc).

♦ Did the children accurately predict which seed had the best parachute?

Talk about/Discuss
♦ Ask what they observed.

♦ What factors might help to determine the size and shape of a seed's parachute?

♦ Encourage the children to suggest reasons why some seeds might not turn into plants.

Science Investigations — 51

Wet Playtimes

100+ Fun Ideas for Transition Time

This book is crammed with stimulating ideas for the awkward, transition times of the day, such as lining-up and answering the register.

The activities have been carefully chosen to ensure pupils work as a team, and develop their self-esteem, physical and mental health, but most importantly, ensure they have fun.

Use these ideas to refresh repetitive routines. If they go smoothly, then the rest of the day will too.

Ages: 5–11yrs   Brilliant

100+ Fun Ideas for

Transition Times

Eileen Jones

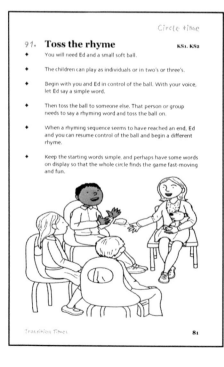

Circle time

91. Toss the rhyme   KS1, KS2

- You will need Ed and a small soft ball.

- The children can play as individuals or in two's or three's.

- Begin with you and Ed in control of the ball. With your voice, let Ed say a simple word.

- Then toss the ball to someone else. That person or group needs to say a rhyming word and toss the ball on.

- When a rhyming sequence seems to have reached an end, Ed and you can resume control of the ball and begin a different rhyme.

- Keep the starting words simple, and perhaps have some words on display so that the whole circle finds the game fast-moving and fun.

Transition Times   **81**

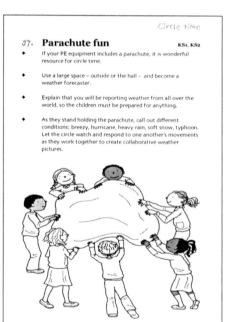

Circle time

37. Parachute fun   KS1, KS2

- If your PE equipment includes a parachute, it is wonderful resource for circle time.

- Use a large space – outside or the hall – and become a weather forecaster.

- Explain that you will be reporting weather from all over the world, so the children must be prepared for anything.

- As they stand holding the parachute, call out different conditions: breezy, hurricane, heavy rain, soft snow, typhoon. Let the circle watch and respond to one another's movements as they work together to create collaborative weather pictures.

Transition Times   77

Wet Playtimes

Lightning Source UK Ltd.
Milton Keynes UK
UKOW030305180112

185571UK00001B/33/P